The Ultimate Dip, Dressing & Sauce RECIPE BOOK

By
Les Ilagan

Les Ilagan

Copyright © CONTENT ARCADE PUBLISHING. All rights reserved.

This cookbook is copyright protected and meant for personal use only.

No part of this cookbook may be used, paraphrased, reproduced, scanned, distributed or sold in any printed or electronic form without permission of the author and the publishing company. Copying pages or any part of this book for any purpose other than own personal use is prohibited and would also mean violation of copyright law.

DISCLAIMER

Content Arcade Publishing and its authors are joined together in their efforts in creating these pages and their publications. Content Arcade Publishing and its authors make no assurance of any kind, stated or implied, with respect to the information provided.

LIMITS OF LIABILITY

Content Arcade Publishing and its authors shall not be held legally responsible in the event of incidental or consequential damages in line with, or arising out of, the supplying of the information presented here.

Table of Contents

Introduction 7

Dips 9

Homemade Baba Ghanoush (Ghannouj) 9
Easy Beetroot Dip....................................12
Classic Fresh Salsa Dip 14
Cream Cheese, Corn, and Cherry Tomato Dip...16
Creamy Hummus with Cayenne Pepper...18
The Classic Queso Dip with Pimiento 21
The Ultimate Greek Tzatziki Dip.......23
Delicious Homemade Guacamole......26
Homemade Remoulade with Fresh Herbs 28
Easy Marjoram Ranch..........................30
Dill and Cucumber Dip 32
Spinach, Artichoke, and Yogurt Dip..34
Traditional Aïoli Dip.............................36
Mayonnaise with Ginger and Green Onion Dip...38
Homemade Nuoc Cham 40
Homemade Sour Cream and Dill Dip 42

Dip Dressing and Sauce

Dressings..**44**

    Classic Mayonnaise Recipe 44
    Roasted Garlic Mayonnaise with Turmeric Powder 46
    Homemade Thousand Island Dressing 48
    Easy Coleslaw Dressing 50
    Lemon and Herb Vinaigrette...............52
    Yummy Orange Vinaigrette.................54
    Homemade Mango Vinaigrette 56
    Parsley and Lemon Dressing...............58
    Homemade Russian Dressing 60
    Soy Vinegar and Sesame Seed Dressing 62
    Mustard Yogurt Dressing....................64
    Curry Mayo Dressing 66

Sauces..**68**

    The Ultimate Basil Pesto Sauce 68
    Homemade Creamy Carbonara Sauce 70
    Easy Homemade Hollandaise Sauce .72
    Easy Homemade Pizza Sauce 74
    Homemade Chicken Gravy 76
    Homemade Chili Sauce.........................78
    Tomato and Basil Pasta Sauce 80
    Homemade White Sauce 82

Homemade Satay Sauce 84
Easy Homemade Lemon Butter Sauce
....86
Steak Sauce Home-Style 88
Classic Homemade Barbecue Sauce..90
Sweet and Spicy Sauce Asian-Style ...92
Homemade Teriyaki Sauce..................94
Spicy Mexican Cheese Sauce...............96
Delicious Cherry Merlot Sauce 98
Homemade Cranberry Sauce 100
Homemade Caramel Sauce...............102
Luscious Strawberry Sauce 104
Sweet Raspberry-Orange Sauce 106
Chocolate Hot Fudge Sauce...............108
Homemade Applesauce......................110

INTRODUCTION

Food on its own can get a little dry and would taste bland without adequate seasoning. What most people would do to remedy, is to make sauces to accompany them. It's very rare to see someone eat barbecue or grilled meat without a bit of BBQ sauce, after all.

Same goes with salads, drizzling the right amount of dressing can make a huge difference to your tossed vegetable salad. As for common snacks like chips, breads, and veggie sticks, dips come in handy to enhance the flavors that are already there.

Yes, these three types of condiments are very important to learn because they can definitely make your dishes taste even better.

This book provides you 50 different recipes that will aid you in making the perfect dinner, snack, or whatever type of meal you are planning to have. With the easy-to-follow steps and a few basic ingredients, you'll find that working with these recipes could be a breeze.

Make your own, homemade mayonnaise, vinaigrettes, pizza or pasta sauces and a lot more! From savory to something sweet, this books has it all! There are many options and we guarantee you that each and every one of them are great!

So sit back, browse through the pages to get an overview of what this book offers, or simply find the recipe that you might want to try for your next meal.

This book is a part of many cookbook series that I am writing, I hope you have fun trying all the recipes in this book.

So now, let's get it started!

Dip Dressing and Sauce

Dips

Homemade Baba Ghanoush (Ghannouj)

A Middle Eastern-inspired eggplant dip best served with pita bread or crackers.

Preparation time: 10 minutes
Total time: 45 minutes
Yield: 6servings

Ingredients
1 large eggplant

1 1/2 tablespoons of tahini sauce
4 cloves of garlic (mashed)
1/2 medium lemon, juiced
pinch of salt
pinch of freshly ground black pepper
1 tablespoon of olive oil
1/2 teaspoon of paprika
fresh parsley, for garnish

Method

1. Preheat your oven to 400 F. Put one oven rack at the top and one at the bottom.

2. Split the eggplant on the side and put it in a casserole dish or baking dish. Put the eggplant on the bottom rack in the oven for 40 minutes or until it shrinks, then switch it up to the top rack. Bake until it looks charred. Allow to cool so you can handle it.

3. Peel the eggplant and place it in a bowl. Add the tahini sauce, garlic, and lemon juice. Mix everything together so that it'll be thoroughly

Dip Dressing and Sauce

mixed. Season with salt and pepper, to taste.

4. Drizzle with some olive oil on top. Sprinkle with paprika and garnish with parsley.

5. Serve and enjoy.

♦♦♦♦♦♦♦♦♦

Easy Beetroot Dip

Totally delicious! Keep this in the fridge beforehand to enhance its flavor.

Preparation Time: 10 minutes
Total Time: 10 minutes
Yield: 8 servings

Ingredients

1 ½ pound beetroot, boiled and cut into small pieces
2 cloves garlic
¼ cup of red wine vinegar
2 tablespoons of extra virgin olive oil
1/2 teaspoon of coriander, ground
1/2 teaspoon of cumin, ground

1/2 teaspoon of sweet paprika
1/4 teaspoon of cinnamon, ground
salt and pepper, to taste

Method
1. Take all of the ingredients and put them in a food processor or blender. Process for 1 minute or until smooth.
2. Serve with warm bread. Pita is recommended.
3. Enjoy.

♦♦♦♦♦♦♦♦♦

Les Ilagan

Classic Fresh Salsa Dip

This delicious classic dip recipe goes really well with chips of any kind.

Preparation time: 15 minutes
Total time: 15 minutes
Yield: 6 servings

Ingredients

1 cup of tomatoes, chopped
1/2 cup of onions, chopped
1/4 cup of green bell pepper, chopped
1/4 cup of cilantro, minced

2 tablespoons of lime juice
1tablespoon of chopped jalapeno pepper, chopped
1/2 teaspoon of cumin, ground
1/4 teaspoon of salt
1/4 teaspoon of ground black pepper

Method

1. Combine all the ingredients in a bowl, mix them together really well.

2. Serve the dip with chips.

3. Enjoy.

◆◆◆◆◆◆◆◆◆

Cream Cheese, Corn, and Cherry Tomato Dip

This creamy dip goes well with anything, really. Serve it with dinner rolls or chips.

Preparation time: 10 minutes
Total Time: 10 minutes
Yield: 6-8 servings

Ingredients

1 package of cream cheese
1/2 cup sour cream

1 cup of cherry tomatoes (sliced in half)
3/4 cup of corn kernels (drained)
1/4 cup of chives (chopped)
salt and pepper, to taste

Method

1. Beat cream cheese and sour cream until smooth.

2. Add the cherry tomatoes, corn kernels, and chives. Season with salt and pepper, to taste. Mix well.

3. Serve and enjoy.

♦♦♦♦♦♦♦♦♦

Les Ilagan

Creamy Hummus with Cayenne Pepper

A nice, spicy take on this classic favorite. Hummus means "chickpeas" in Arabic. This dip is famous all over the world, perfect for parties!

Preparation time: 10 minutes
Total time: 10 minutes
Yield: 8 servings

Ingredients

1 can of chickpeas (reserve half of the liquid)

Dip Dressing and Sauce

2 cloves of garlic
4 tablespoons of lemon juice
2 tablespoons of tahini sauce
½ teaspoon cayenne pepper
¼ teaspoon of salt
¼ teaspoon of black pepper
2 tablespoons of olive oil
½ teaspoon sweet paprika

Method

1. Process the chickpeas and garlic together in a food processor (you may want to save some chickpeas for garnishing).

2. Add the lemon juice, tahini sauce, and cayenne pepper. Season with salt and pepper to taste. Blend everything together until you get a creamy consistency.

3. Transfer your chickpea mixture into a bowl. Make a well in the center and pour a generous amount of olive oil in it.

4. Top the hummus with whole chickpeas and sprinkle with paprika.

5. Serve with pita or similar breads.

6. Enjoy.

◆◆◆◆◆◆◆◆◆

Dip Dressing and Sauce

The Classic Queso Dip with Pimiento

Take out your tortilla chips! This classic dip is perfect for get-togethers. Your friends will surely ask you for this recipe.

Preparation Time: 10 minutes
Total Time: 10 minutes
Yield: 10-12 servings

Ingredients

1 tablespoon of butter
1 tablespoon of cornstarch
3/4 cup of sour cream
1 cup of shredded Cheddar cheese

¼ cup of pimiento, chopped

Method
1. Melt the butter in a saucepan over medium heat. Stir in the cornstarch then add the sour cream.

2. Once the mixture is bubbling, you can add in the cheddar cheese and the pimiento. Stir some more until everything has come together smoothly and the cheese has melted. It should take about 7-10 minutes for the mixture to thicken.

3. Serve the dip while it's hot.

4. Enjoy.

♦♦♦♦♦♦♦♦

Dip Dressing and Sauce

The Ultimate Greek Tzatziki Dip

You can serve fried food and more with this easy-to-prepare dip! The taste of cucumbers blend well with the creaminess of yogurt, leaving a very refreshing taste in your mouth!

Preparation time: 10 minutes
Total time: 10 minutes
Yield: 8 servings

Ingredients

2(6 oz.) containers of plain yogurt

1/2 of a cucumber with its peel (grated)
1 clove of garlic (pressed)
2 tablespoons of lemon juice
2 tablespoons of extra-virgin olive oil
1 teaspoon of lemon zest (finely grated)
1 tablespoon of fresh dill (chopped)
salt and black pepper, to taste

Method

1. Take a large bowl and whisk together the yogurt, garlic, olive oil, lemon juice, and the cucumber.
2. Once combined, you can add the lemon zest and dill. Season with salt and pepper, to taste. Stir everything together until it becomes smooth.
3. Pour into ramekins or what have you, cover tightly with cling wrap then refrigerate for a while before serving.

Dip Dressing and Sauce

4. Enjoy.

◆◆◆◆◆◆◆◆

Les Ilagan

Delicious Homemade Guacamole

This delicious avocado dip will earn a spot in your party menu. You can mash the avocados to be really smooth, or you can leave them chunky.

Preparation time: 10 minutes
Total time: 10 minutes
Yield: 8 servings

Ingredients

2 medium avocados (peeled, pitted, and mashed to your desired consistency)
1 medium lime (juiced)
2 medium tomatoes (diced)
1/2 cup of onion (diced)
3 tablespoons of cilantro (chopped)
1 teaspoon of garlic (minced)
1/4 teaspoon of salt
1/4 teaspoon black pepper

Method

1. Combine the mashed avocados with lime juice then add in the tomatoes, onion, cilantro, and garlic. Season with salt and pepper, to taste.
2. Cover and refrigerate until ready to serve.

♦♦♦♦♦♦♦♦

Homemade Remoulade with Fresh Herbs

Cut the herbs finely if you want a very smooth texture. Let it rest in the fridge before serving for optimal taste.

Preparation time: 10 minutes
Total time: 10 minutes
Yield: 8 servings

Ingredients
1 cup of mayonnaise

Dip Dressing and Sauce

2 tablespoons of mustard
2 tablespoons of ketchup
1 tablespoon of lemon juice
1 tablespoon of Worcestershire sauce
2 tablespoons of scallion (chopped)
1 stalk of celery (chopped)
1 tablespoon of fresh tarragon (chopped)
2 cloves of garlic (minced)
1 teaspoon of sweet paprika
2 teaspoons of hot sauce
salt and pepper

Method

1. Take your condiments. Whisk them together in a large bowl.
2. Add the herbs and the spices, then the lemon juice. Season with salt and pepper, to taste. Mix well.
3. Refrigerate until ready to serve.

♦♦♦♦♦♦♦♦♦

Les Ilagan

Easy Marjoram Ranch

Can be used as a dip or as a dressing. You'll find that this recipe will become highly requested at parties!

Preparation time: 10 minutes
Total time: 10 minutes
Yield: 6servings

Ingredients
1 cup of mayonnaise
1/2 teaspoon of garlic powder
1/2 teaspoon of onion powder
2 teaspoons of chopped parsley
2 teaspoons of marjoram

Dip Dressing and Sauce

1/2 cup of unsweetened soy milk
1/4 teaspoon freshly ground black pepper

Method

1. Mix all the ingredients together in a bowl thoroughly.
2. Refrigerate until ready to serve.

   Tip: This recipe goes well with cucumbers and greens such as lettuce.

♦♦♦♦♦♦♦♦♦

Dill and Cucumber Dip

Add a fresh flavor to your grilled dishes with this dill and cucumber combination.

Preparation time: 5 minutes
Total time: 5 minutes
Yield: 8-10 servings

Ingredients

1 package of cream cheese
1/4 cup sour cream
1 medium cucumber (grated or finely chopped)

1/4 cup of Swiss cheese (finely grated)
1 tablespoon of lemon juice
1/2 teaspoon of dill
1/4 teaspoon of minced garlic
1/4 teaspoon of freshly ground black pepper

Method

1. Whisk together cream cheese and sour cream until smooth.
2. Add the cucumber, Swiss cheese, lemon juice, dill, and garlic. Mix well. Season with pepper, to taste.
3. Cover the bowl with cling wrap, chill until ready to serve.
4. Enjoy.

◆◆◆◆◆◆◆◆◆

Spinach, Artichoke, and Yogurt Dip

Serve with bread or anything else you can think of! This is a very healthy and delicious dip.

Preparation time: 10 minutes
Total time: 10 minutes
Yield: 24 servings

Ingredients

1 bag of fresh spinach (finely chopped)
1 can of artichoke hearts (drained and chopped)
1 can of water chestnuts (chopped)

Dip Dressing and Sauce

2 cups of plain yogurt
1/4 cup of grated Parmesan cheese
pinch of ground black pepper
pinch of garlic powder
pinch of onion powder

Method

1. Put the chopped spinach with the artichoke hearts and water chestnuts in a medium bowl.
2. Add the yogurt, Parmesan cheese, and the seasonings. Stir together until mixed well.
3. Serve and consume immediately or refrigerate until ready to serve.

◆◆◆◆◆◆◆◆◆

Traditional Aïoli Dip

This is a type of mayonnaise made using pureed garlic cloves as a base.

Preparation time: 5 minutes
Total time: 5 minutes
Yield: 12 servings

Ingredients

6 cloves of garlic
salt and black pepper
2 egg yolks
1 teaspoon of Dijon mustard
1 cup of olive oil
1 1/2 tablespoons of lemon juice

Method

1. Put the garlic in a bowl and throw in a pinch of salt. Crush them together into a paste. Stir in the egg yolks and the mustard. Mix well.
2. Stir in the oil, a few drops at a time, while stirring slowly. Once half of the oil has been incorporated, add about half of the lemon juice. The remaining oil can now be added a little more quickly, but you still have to stir the mixture slowly. Finally, add the remaining lemon juice.
3. Serve immediately or refrigerate until ready to serve.

♦♦♦♦♦♦♦♦♦

Les Ilagan

Mayonnaise with Ginger and Green Onion Dip

This fantastic recipe can be used for dipping or for dressing vegetable salads.

Preparation time: 10 minutes
Total time: 10 minutes
Yield: 1 cup

Ingredients

2 egg yolks
1/2 teaspoon of ginger juice
3/4 cup of olive oil

Dip Dressing and Sauce

1/4 cup of peanut oil
2 tablespoons of green onions (chopped)
salt and ground black pepper

Method

1. In a food processor, blend the egg yolks, salt, and 1/2 teaspoon of ginger juice. Do this briefly. While the motor is running, slowly add the oils in.

2. Add the green onions. Season with salt and black pepper. Add more ginger juice, if desired.

3. Serve and enjoy.

♦♦♦♦♦♦♦♦♦

Homemade Nuoc Cham

This traditional Vietnamese dip packs a whole lot of flavor. A bit sweet, but mostly savory, this dip goes well with rice-paper spring rolls.

Preparation Time: 5 minutes
Total Time: 5 minutes
Yield: 10-12 servings

Ingredients
1/2 medium lemon (juiced)
1/2 cup of warm water
1/3 cup of white vinegar
1/4 cup of fish sauce
2 tablespoons of white sugar

Dip Dressing and Sauce

3 cloves of garlic (minced)
3 Thai chili peppers (chopped)
1 green onion (finely chopped)

Method
1. In a small bowl, combine lemon, warm water, white vinegar, fish sauce, sugar, garlic, chili peppers, and the green onion. Mix until combined well.
2. Serve and enjoy.

♦♦♦♦♦♦♦♦

Homemade Sour Cream and Dill Dip

Creamy, soft, and has pops of color thanks to the dill. Serve this with a bunch of carrot sticks, cauliflower, and celery.

Preparation time: 5 minutes
Total time: 5 minutes
Yield: 1 cup

Ingredients

1 cup of sour cream
2 tablespoons of onion (finely chopped)

1 teaspoons of fresh dill weed (chopped)
1 teaspoon of white sugar
salt and pepper

Method

1. Whisk together the mayonnaise and sour cream.

2. Add the chopped onion, dill, and white sugar. Season with salt and pepper, to taste.

3. Cover and refrigerate before serving.

♦♦♦♦♦♦♦♦♦

Dressings

Classic Mayonnaise Recipe

For best results, have all the ingredients at room temperature before starting to work on this classic recipe.

Preparation time: 20 minutes
Total Time: 20 minutes
Yield: 1 cup

Ingredients
2 egg yolks

Dip Dressing and Sauce

2 tablespoons of vinegar
1 teaspoon of Dijon mustard
1 cup of canola oil
salt and pepper, to taste

Method

1. Put the egg yolks into a bowl. Stir in half of the vinegar and, then the mustard.
2. Add the oil, drop by drop, mixing constantly. Once half of the oil has been incorporated, you may add the rest a little quicker. Continue to whisk until the sauce is thick, shiny, and smooth.
3. Mix in the remaining vinegar and add more mustard, if desired. Season with salt and pepper, to taste.
4. Serve and enjoy.

♦♦♦♦♦♦♦♦♦

Roasted Garlic Mayonnaise with Turmeric Powder

Enjoy dipping vegetables and fried food into this very tasty homemade mayonnaise.

Preparation time: 10 minutes
Total time: 20 minutes
Yield: 1 cup

Ingredients
2 cloves of roasted garlic
2 tablespoons of olive oil
2 egg yolks

Dip Dressing and Sauce

3 teaspoons of lemon juice
1 cup of olive oil
1/2 teaspoon turmeric powder, to taste
1/4 teaspoon salt
1/4 teaspoon ground black pepper

Method

1. Gently squeeze the garlic cloves out of their skins. Put them in a bowl and add in the egg yolks with 1 teaspoon of lemon juice. Mix together well.

2. Stir in the olive oil, one drop at a time, until everything has been used. Add one more teaspoon of lemon juice and turmeric powder. Season with salt and pepper. Mix until combined well.

3. Serve and enjoy.

Tip: You can add more lemon juice, if desired.

♦♦♦♦♦♦♦♦

Homemade Thousand Island Dressing

Kids and adults alike will absolutely love this dressing. It's a very popular one and is often served with vegetable salads.

Preparation Time: 10 minutes
Total Time: 10 minutes
Yield: 1 ¼ cups

Ingredients
1 cup of mayonnaise (bottled or homemade)
2 tablespoons pickle relish
1 tablespoon of green pepper (chopped)
1 tablespoon of chives (finely chopped)

Dip Dressing and Sauce

1 hard-boiled egg (chopped)
a few drops of hot sauce
salt and ground black pepper

Method

1. Put the mayonnaise into a medium bowl.
2. Stir in the remaining ingredients.
3. Serve and enjoy.

♦♦♦♦♦♦♦♦♦

Easy Coleslaw Dressing

Bring more flavor to your main course with coleslaw slathered with this tasty dressing.

Preparation Time: 5 minutes
Total Time: 5 minutes
Yield: 1 cup

Ingredients

1/2 cup of sour cream
1/2 cup of mayonnaise
2 tablespoons of cider vinegar
1 teaspoon of mustard powder
2 teaspoons of caraway seeds, ground
pinch of caster sugar
salt and ground black pepper, to taste

Method

1. Combine the sour cream, mayonnaise, vinegar, mustard powder, and the caraway seeds in a bowl. Mix them together thoroughly.
2. Add sugar and seasonings to taste.
3. Serve and enjoy.

◆◆◆◆◆◆◆◆

Lemon and Herb Vinaigrette

Add the herbs just before serving so that they don't darken. Choose the kind of herb that suits the food you're going to put the vinaigrette on.

Preparation time: 5 minutes
Total time: 5 minutes
Yield: ¾ cup

Ingredients

¼ cup of lemon juice
1 tablespoon of Dijon mustard
½ cup of olive oil

Dip Dressing and Sauce

2 tablespoons of chopped rosemary
salt and pepper, to taste

Method

1. Combine the lemon juice and mustard in a bowl.
2. Pour in the oil in a thin, steady stream. Whisk everything together until the vinaigrette is blended and thick. Season with salt and pepper, to taste.
3. Add the chopped rosemary. Mix well.
4. Serve and enjoy.

♦♦♦♦♦♦♦♦

Les Ilagan

Yummy Orange Vinaigrette

This dressing works well with grated carrot salad or beetroots. Exquisitely refreshing and lends just the right amount of sweetness.

Preparation time: 5 minutes
Total time: 5 minutes
Yield: 3/4 cup

Ingredients

¼ cup of freshly squeezed orange juice
1 teaspoon of orange zest (finely grated
1 tablespoon of red wine vinegar

Dip Dressing and Sauce

1 tablespoon of balsamic vinegar
1 shallot (finely chopped)
½ cup of olive oil
½ teaspoon sesame seeds
salt and pepper, to taste

Method

1. Combine the orange juice and zest, red wine vinegar, balsamic vinegar, shallot, and sesame seeds in a bowl.

2. Stir in the oil slowly, whisking until the mixture is well blended. Season with salt and pepper to taste.

3. Serve and enjoy.

♦♦♦♦♦♦♦♦♦

Homemade Mango Vinaigrette

This goes really well with smoked salmon, chicken, or turkey. Serve with potatoes or salad to complete the meal.

Preparation time: 10 minutes
Total time: 10 minutes
Yield: 1 cup

Ingredients

1 ripe mango (peeled and sliced)
2 tablespoons of red wine vinegar

Dip Dressing and Sauce

1/2 cup of olive oil
salt and pepper

Method

1. Combine the mango, red wine vinegar, and olive oil in a blender or food processor and blend until smooth. Season with salt and pepper, to taste.

2. Serve and enjoy.

◆◆◆◆◆◆◆◆◆

Parsley and Lemon Dressing

Make this dressing a few hours before serving. Toss with Romaine lettuce and croutons for a quick, easy, and tasty salad.

Preparation time: 5 minutes
Total time: 5 minutes
Yield: 1 cup

Ingredients

1 cup of olive oil
2 tablespoons of lemon juice
1 teaspoon of lemon zest (finely grated)
2 cloves of garlic (finely chopped)

1 1/2 tablespoon of Parmesan cheese (grated)
salt and pepper, to taste

Method

1. Take all of the ingredients and put them in a small bowl. Stir until well blended.
2. Best served with tossed green salad.
3. Enjoy.

♦♦♦♦♦♦♦♦♦

Les Ilagan

Homemade Russian Dressing

With a hint of spiciness, this dressing will make your salads more exciting.

Preparation time: 5 minutes
Total time: 5 minutes
Yield: 1 ¼ cup

Ingredients

1 cup of mayonnaise
3 tablespoons of tomato sauce
3 tablespoons of chopped gherkins
1 shallot (finely chopped)
1 teaspoon of fresh horseradish (grated)

Dip Dressing and Sauce

a few drops of hot sauce
salt and pepper

Method
1. Place the mayonnaise in a small bowl.
2. Stir in the tomato sauce, gherkins, shallot, horseradish, and hot sauce. Mix well. Season with salt and pepper, to taste.
3. Serve and enjoy.

◆◆◆◆◆◆◆◆◆

Soy Vinegar and Sesame Seed Dressing

This is a really simple dressing perfect for green salad or a dip to poultry.

Preparation time: 5 minutes
Total time: 5 minutes
Yield: 1 ¼ cup

Ingredients
¾ cup of olive oil
¼ cup of rice vinegar
3 tablespoons of white sugar
2 tablespoons of sesame oil
2 tablespoons of soy sauce

Dip Dressing and Sauce

1 tablespoon honey
1 tablespoon of toasted sesame seeds

Method

1. Whisk all the ingredients together in a small bowl.
2. Serve and enjoy.

♦♦♦♦♦♦♦♦♦

Les Ilagan

Mustard Yogurt Dressing

A light dressing for potatoes or spinach salads. Guaranteed to satisfy.

Preparation time: 5 minutes
Total time: 5 minutes
Yield: 1 cup

Ingredients

1 cup of Greek yogurt
1 tablespoon of Dijon mustard
1 tablespoon of parsley (chopped)

1 tablespoon of spring onions (finely chopped)
salt and pepper, to taste

Method

1. Combine the yogurt, mustard, parsley, and green onion into a small bowl. Season with salt and pepper, to taste. Mix well.
2. Cover and chill before using.
3. Enjoy.

♦♦♦♦♦♦♦♦

Curry Mayo Dressing

This sauce is great with green salad ,roasted poultry, fish, and anything else you can think of!

Preparation time: 10 minutes
Total time: 10 minutes
Yield: 1 cup

Ingredients

1 cup of mayonnaise
2 tablespoons of lemon juice
1 teaspoon of curry powder

1 teaspoon of sugar
salt and pepper

Method

1. Mix together mayonnaise, lemon juice, curry powder, and sugar in a serving bowl. Stir until sugar is dissolved completly. Season with salt and pepper, to taste.
2. Serve and enjoy.

♦♦♦♦♦♦♦♦

Les Ilagan

Sauces

The Ultimate Basil Pesto Sauce

Learn how to make the ever-popular pasta sauce with this easy-to-follow recipe!

Preparation time: 10 minutes
Total time: 10 minutes
Yield: 2 cups

Dip Dressing and Sauce

Ingredients
4 cups fresh basil leaves
3 cloves garlic
1/2 cup walnuts
¼ cup pine nuts
¼ cup Parmesan cheese
1 cup of olive oil
salt and black pepper

Method
1. Combine basil, garlic, walnuts, pine nuts, and parmesan cheese in a blender or food processor. Pulse until it forms a paste.

2. Add olive oil bit by bit while motor is running. Season with salt and pepper, to taste.

3. Serve and enjoy.

♦♦♦♦♦♦♦♦

Homemade Creamy Carbonara Sauce

Beautifully rich and decadently creamy, this sauce will make you ask for seconds! If desired, you may add some Parmesan cheese.

Preparation time: 5 minutes
Total time: 15 minutes
Yield: 1 ½ cup

Ingredients
2 medium eggs
1 cup of cream

Dip Dressing and Sauce

1 tablespoon olive oil
1 chopped onion
1 crushed garlic
4 slices of turkey ham
salt and pepper

Method

1. Whisk together the eggs and cream.

2. Heat oil in a small saucepan. Sauté the onion with the garlic and the turkey ham.

3. Add the egg mixture into the pan and bring to a boil. Season with salt and pepper, to taste. Remove from heat.

4. Serve with pasta.

◆◆◆◆◆◆◆◆

Les Ilagan

Easy Homemade Hollandaise Sauce

Make this classic French sauce without the need for a double boiler!

Preparation time: 10 minutes
Total time: 10 minutes
Yield: 2/3 cup

Ingredients

3 large egg yolks
1 tablespoon of lemon juice
½ cup of warm butter, melted

salt and pepper

Method

1. Melt the butter in a saucepan.

2. In a small bowl whisk together the egg and lemon juice. It should lighten in color and this process should only take about 30 seconds.

3. Slowly pour the warm melted butter in. Mix well until all of the butter is thoroughly incorporated. Season with salt and pepper, to taste.

4. Serve.

◆◆◆◆◆◆◆◆

Easy Homemade Pizza Sauce

Wow your party guests with your own pizza sauce! This recipe features easy-to-find ingredients and easy steps. No cooking required.

Preparation time: 5 minutes
Total time: 5 minutes
Yield: 2 cups

Ingredients

1 1/2 cups of tomato sauce
1/2 cup of tomato paste

Dip Dressing and Sauce

1/2 teaspoon of dried oregano
1/2 teaspoon of dried basil
1/2 teaspoon of garlic powder
1/2 teaspoon of ground paprika
1/2 teaspoon of sugar (optional)
salt and pepper

Method

1. Combine the tomato sauce with the tomato paste until it is well blended.
2. Add the oregano, basil, garlic, paprika, and sugar. Season with salt and pepper, to taste.
3. Spread over pizza crusts.
4. Enjoy.

♦♦♦♦♦♦♦♦♦

Homemade Chicken Gravy

A gravy made from chicken stock and heavy cream. Surprise your kids with this delicious gravy.

Preparation time: 5 minutes
Total time: 15 minutes
Yield: 3 cups

Ingredients

2 tablespoons of unsalted butter
1/2 cup of flour
1/4 cup pan drippings from roasted chicken

Dip Dressing and Sauce

2 cups of chicken stock
1/4 cup of heavy cream
salt and ground white pepper, to taste
a pinch of cayenne pepper

Method

1. In a saucepan over medium, melt the butter. Once melted, stir the flour. Cook for 2 minutes.

2. Add the pan drippings and chicken stock. Turn the heat to medium-low and simmer the gravy. Cook until the gravy is thick enough, stirring constantly. This should take about 5 minutes.

3. Stir in the heavy cream and the seasonings. Cook further 2 minutes. Remove from heat. Cool slightly before serving.

♦♦♦♦♦♦♦♦

Les Ilagan

Homemade Chili Sauce

Hot, hot, hot! This chili sauce will give your dishes that kick that you desired.

Preparation time: 5 minutes
Total time: 20 minutes
Yield: 1 cup

Ingredients

1 cup of tomato sauce
3 tablespoons of brown sugar
3 tablespoons of white vinegar
1 teaspoon of lemon juice

Dip Dressing and Sauce

1/2 teaspoon of chili powder
1/2 teaspoon of all-spice
1/2 teaspoon of salt
1/4 teaspoon of garlic powder

Method

1. Combine all of the ingredients in a small saucepan and cook over medium heat.

2. When the mixture starts to bubble, reduce the heat to low. Simmer for about 15 minutes. Remove from heat. Allow to cool.

◆◆◆◆◆◆◆◆◆

Les Ilagan

Tomato and Basil Pasta Sauce

You can use this on both pasta and bread. Really easy to make and definitely delicious.

Preparation time: 5 minutes
Total time: 20 minutes
Yield: 4 servings

Ingredients

2 tablespoons of olive oil
1 cup tomato puree

Dip Dressing and Sauce

2 tablespoons tomato paste
1/4 cup of dry white wine
1/4 cup of chopped fresh basil
1 teaspoon of garlic powder
1/4 teaspoon of salt
1/4 teaspoon of freshly ground black pepper

Method

1. In a skillet over medium-high heat, heat the olive oil. Add in the tomato puree and tomato paste and dry white wine let it cook for 15 minutes.

2. Add the basil, garlic powder, salt, pepper.

3. Serve the sauce with some pasta or bread of your choice.

♦♦♦♦♦♦♦♦

Les Ilagan

Homemade White Sauce

This delicious white sauce can be used as a base for many things; including but not limited to Mac and Cheese sauce. Really simple and easy to make!

Preparation time: 5 minutes
Total time: 15 minutes
Yield: 4 servings

Ingredients

2 tablespoons of butter
2 tablespoons of flour

1 cup of milk
ground mixed spices (optional)
salt and pepper

Method

1. Melt the butter in a saucepan over medium heat. Add the flour and stir until blended well.

2. Slowly pour in the milk while stirring continuously.

3. It's ready once it's thickened. You may add more milk depending on what consistency you want.

4. Sprinkle with the ground mixed spices if desired. Season with salt and pepper, to taste.

◆◆◆◆◆◆◆◆

Les Ilagan

Homemade Satay Sauce

Serve over grilled chicken skewers with this Satay sauce and garnish with lime wedges for a satisfying meal!

Preparation time: 5 minutes
Total time: 15 minutes
Yield: 8 servings

Ingredients
4 ounces of roasted unsalted peanuts
1 clove of garlic (minced)
2 tablespoons of red curry paste

1 1/2 cups of coconut milk
2 tablespoons of sugar
1/2 medium lime (juiced)
1/4teaspoon hot chili pepper, minced
salt and pepper

Method

1. Combine the peanuts, garlic, curry paste, and some of the coconut milk in a food processor or blender. Puree these ingredients. Add the remaining coconut milk and the sugar. Mix together until smooth.

2. Pour this mixture into a saucepan along with the lime juice and chili. Boil it for about 2-3 minutes. Reduce heat to a simmer and cook further 5-7 minutes, stirring occasionally. Season with salt and pepper, to taste.

♦♦♦♦♦♦♦♦♦

Les Ilagan

Easy Homemade Lemon Butter Sauce

Pour this over any seafood for added taste. This is a really simple, but powerful sauce.

Preparation time: 5 minutes
Total time: 10 minutes
Yield: 4 servings

Ingredients

1/2cup of butter
1/4 cup of lemon juice
1 teaspoon of Worcestershire sauce

Dip Dressing and Sauce

chopped fresh herbs (rosemary, dill, thyme, sage, parsley)
salt and pepper

Method

1. Melt the butter in a small saucepan over medium heat.
2. Add the lemon juice, Worcestershire sauce, and herbs. Cook further 2 minutes. Season with salt and pepper, to taste.
3. Add herbs for garnish and added taste. Pour over fish or other seafood and enjoy.

♦♦♦♦♦♦♦♦♦

Les Ilagan

Steak Sauce Home-Style

This is a great tasting sauce for your steaks, burgers, and fries.

Preparation time: 5 minutes
Total time: 5 minutes
Yield: 10-12 servings

Ingredients

1 1/4 cups ketchup
2 tablespoons Worcestershire sauce
2 tablespoons prepared yellow mustard
1 1/2 tablespoons apple cider vinegar

Dip Dressing and Sauce

3-4 drops hot pepper sauce
1/2 teaspoon Kosher salt
1/2 teaspoon freshly ground black pepper

Method

1. In a medium bowl, whisk together the ketchup, Worcestershire sauce, mustard, apple cider vinegar, hot pepper sauce, salt and pepper.

2. Transfer to a jar with lid. Seal tightly.

3. Refrigerate until ready to use.

♦♦♦♦♦♦♦♦♦

Classic Homemade Barbecue Sauce

Perfect sauce for grilled meat or poultry. Delicious and a little spicy, just what you need for outdoor barbecue parties.

Preparation time: 5 minutes
Total time: 15 minutes
Yield: 2 2/3 cups

Ingredients

1 cup of tomato sauce
1/4cup of tomato paste

Dip Dressing and Sauce

1/4 cup of butter
1/4 cup of Worcestershire sauce
1/4 cup of packed brown sugar
1/4 cup of molasses
1/4 cup of apple cider vinegar
2 1/2 teaspoons of balsamic vinegar
1 tablespoon of mustard
1 teaspoon of chili powder
1/2 teaspoon of onion powder
1/2 teaspoon of garlic powder

Method

1. Combine the tomato sauce, tomato paste, butter, Worcestershire sauce, brown sugar, molasses, apple cider vinegars, balsamic vinegar, and mustard in a medium saucepan. Cook over medium heat for 7-10 minutes, stirring often.
2. Stir in the seasonings. Cook further 1-2 minutes. Allow to cool.
3. Transfer to a jar with lid. Seal tightly.
4. Refrigerate until ready to use.

♦♦♦♦♦♦♦♦♦

Les Ilagan

Sweet and Spicy Sauce Asian-Style

Goes well with almost anything, from noodles to spring rolls. Make your dish pop with the sweet and spicy flavor of this sauce.

Preparation Time: 5 minutes
Total Time: 10 minutes
Yield: 3 cups

Ingredients

1 cup of rice vinegar
3/4 cup of sugar
1/2 cup of ketchup

Dip Dressing and Sauce

1 teaspoon of garlic (minced)
2 teaspoons of red hot chili pepper (minced)
1 tablespoon of cornstarch + 1 cup of water
salt and pepper

Method

1. Whisk together cornstarch and water in a small bowl until dissolved. Set aside.
2. In a saucepan over high heat, bring the vinegar to a boil. Add in the sugar, ketchup, garlic, and chili. Allow to simmer for 5 minutes then stir in the cornstarch mixture. Season with salt and pepper, to taste.
3. Remove from heat and allow to cool before serving.

◆◆◆◆◆◆◆◆

Homemade Teriyaki Sauce

This is the probably the best teriyaki sauce that you will ever have.

Preparation time: 10 minutes
Total time: 30 minutes
Yield: 1 2/3 cups

Ingredients

2/3 cup mirin (Japanese sweet rice wine)
1 cup soy sauce
2 tablespoons rice wine
1/3 cup brown sugar

5 cloves garlic(minced)
1 shallot (minced)
1 tablespoon fresh ginger (minced)
1/2 teaspoon red pepper flakes
1/4 teaspoon freshly ground black pepper
1 teaspoon sesame oil

Method

1. Bring mirin to a boil in a medium saucepan over medium-high heat. Cook for 3-5 minutes.
2. Stir in the soy sauce, rice wine vinegar, brown sugar, garlic, shallot, ginger, pepper flakes, and black pepper.Cook further 5 minutes. Add sesame oil and stir well. Remove from heat. Allow to cool
3. Store in a tightly sealed jar in the refrigerator.

◆◆◆◆◆◆◆◆

Spicy Mexican Cheese Sauce

Friends would want to ask you for this recipe. It brings life to your tortilla platter or favorite tacos because of that added zing!

Preparation time: 5 minutes
Total time: 10 minutes
Yield: 2 ½ cups

Ingredients
1 jalapeno pepper
2 cups of shredded cheddar cheese
1/2 cup of milk

2 teaspoons of paprika
1 teaspoon of garlic powder
1/2 teaspoon of black pepper

Method

1. Chop your jalapeno into very small pieces. Include the seeds for added heat. Set aside and turn the stove on to medium heat.

2. Melt your cheese with the milk and the chopped jalapeno in a medium saucepan. Watch it carefully because it might overflow. Stir in the garlic powder, paprika, and pepper. Once the cheese has melted, you can turn the stove off.

3. Pour the cheese sauce into a serving bowl. Allow to cool.

4. Serve with tortilla chips or tacos and enjoy.

◆◆◆◆◆◆◆◆

Delicious Cherry Merlot Sauce

This sweet sauce complements most roasted meat or poultry dishes. Really easy to make and totally delicious.

Preparation time: 5 minutes
Total time: 15 minutes
Yield: 2 cups

Ingredients

1 pound pitted cherries
1/2 cup water
2/3 cup of sugar

1/3 cup Merlot wine
2 tablespoons of lemon juice

Method

1. Put the pitted cherries, water and sugar in a medium saucepan. Bring the mixture to a boil over medium-high heat, stirring often.

2. Add the Merlot. Reduce heat and simmer for 10 minutes. Remove it from heat and then finally stir in the lemon juice. Allow to cool.

3. Serve and enjoy.

◆◆◆◆◆◆◆◆

Homemade Cranberry Sauce

This traditional sauce can be used on roasted poultry or meat.

Preparation Time: 15 minutes
Total Time: 15 minutes
Yield: 10-12 servings

Ingredients
12 ounces of fresh cranberries
1 cup of white sugar
1 cup of orange juice

Method

1. Dissolve the sugar with the orange juice in a saucepan over medium heat. Stir in the cranberries and cook for 15 minutes.
2. Remove from heat. Transfer the sauce into a bowl. The sauce should thicken as it cools.
3. Serve with roasted turkey, chicken or meat.
4. Enjoy.

◆◆◆◆◆◆◆◆◆

Les Ilagan

Homemade Caramel Sauce

Perfect as a topping for cake or ice cream. Make this and fulfill your sweet cravings.

Preparation time: 5 minutes
Total time: 10 minutes
Yield: 2 1/4 cups

Ingredients
1 1/4 cups of sugar
1/3 cup of water
3/4 cup of whipping cream
1/3 cup of butter (cut into small pieces)
1/2 teaspoon of vanilla extract

Method

1. In a medium saucepan, dissolve the sugar over medium-low heat, stirring often.

2. Increase the heat to medium-high. Bring to a boil and cook until amber in color and thickened.

3. Add the cream slowly, then the butter. Stir until it becomes smooth and resembles caramel. Remove from heat and then add the vanilla extract.

♦♦♦♦♦♦♦♦♦

Luscious Strawberry Sauce

Especially good on cheesecakes and other desserts, this awesome berry sauce is full of flavor and sweetness.

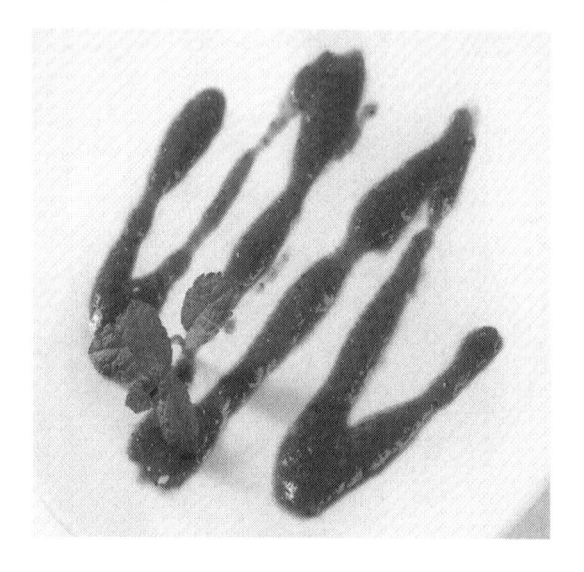

Preparation time: 5 minutes
Total time: 20 minutes
Yield: 2 cups

Ingredients
1 1/2 pounds of fresh hulled fresh strawberries (pureed)

3/4 cup of white sugar
1/2cup + 1/4 cup water, divided
2 tablespoons of balsamic vinegar
1 teaspoon of cornstarch

Method

1. Combine the strawberry puree, sugar, ½ cup water, and balsamic vinegar in a medium saucepan and cook over medium heat. Reduce the heat to medium-low, cover and simmer for 10 more minutes.
2. In a small bowl, combine the remaining ¼ cup water and the cornstarch.
3. Add the cornstarch mixture into the strawberries. Cook and stir constantly until the mixture thickens then remove from heat. Allow to cool.
4. Transfer in a jar with lid. Refrigerate until ready to use.

◆◆◆◆◆◆◆◆

Les Ilagan

Sweet Raspberry-Orange Sauce

Like the strawberry sauce, this sauce suits cheesecakes and other desserts very well.

Preparation time: 5 minutes
Total time: 20 minutes
Yield: 4 cups

Ingredients

1 1/2 pounds of fresh hulled fresh raspberries (pureed)

3/4 cup of white sugar
1/2 cup fresh orange juice
1/4 cup water
1 teaspoon of cornstarch

Method

1. Combine the pureed raspberries, sugar, and orange juice in a medium saucepan. Cook over medium heat. Reduce the heat to medium-low, cover and simmer for 10 more minutes.
2. In a small bowl, combine water and cornstarch.
3. Add the cornstarch mixture into the raspberry sauce. Cook and stir constantly until the mixture thickens then remove from heat. Allow to cool.
4. Transfer in a jar with lid. Refrigerate until ready to use.

♦♦♦♦♦♦♦♦

Chocolate Hot Fudge Sauce

This decadent chocolate sauce can be poured over ice cream or brownies for that added oomph!

Preparation time: 5 minutes
Total time: 15 minutes
Yield: 2 ¼ cup

Ingredients

4 squares of unsweetened chocolate
1 cup of heavy cream
1 cup of white sugar

1 tablespoon of butter
1/2 teaspoon of vanilla extract

Method

1. Combine the chocolate and cream in a saucepan over medium heat, stirring frequently, to melt it.
2. Add the sugar and butter. Cook, stirring until sugar is dissolved completely. Once smooth, heat some more without boiling. Remove from heat and add in the vanilla. Allow to cool.
3. Enjoy.

♦♦♦♦♦♦♦♦

Les Ilagan

Homemade Applesauce

Make this delicious treat with just three main ingredients.

Preparation time: 5 minutes
Total time: 20 minutes
Yield: 6 servings

Ingredients
4 cooking apples (peeled, cored, and chopped)
3/4 cup of water
1/4 cup of white sugar
1/2 teaspoon of ground cinnamon

Dip Dressing and Sauce

1 tablespoon butter

Method

1. Combine the apples with the water, cinnamon, and sugar in a saucepan. Cover and allow to cook over medium heat for 15 minutes or until very tender and mushy.

2. Gently mash with a fork or potato masher. Stir in butter and cook further 2 minutes. Allow to cool.

♦♦♦♦♦♦♦♦

Printed in Great Britain
by Amazon